Great Empires

The Mesopotamian Empires

ELLIS ROXBURGH

Cavendish
Square

New York

Published in 2016 by Cavendish Square Publishing, LLC
243 5th Avenue, Suite 136, New York, NY 10016

© 2016 Brown Bear Books Ltd

First Edition

Website: cavendishsq.com

CPSIA Compliance Information: Batch #WS15CSQ

Library of Congress Cataloging-in-Publication Data

Roxburgh, Ellis.
The Mesopotamian empires / Ellis Roxburgh.
pages cm. — (Great empires)
Includes bibliographical references and index.
ISBN 978-1-50260-630-3 (hardcover) ISBN 978-1-50260-631-0 (ebook)
1. Iraq—Civilization—To 634—Juvenile literature. I. Title.

DS69.5.R69 2016
935—dc23

2015004966

For Brown Bear Books Ltd:
Editorial Director: Lindsey Lowe
Managing Editor: Tim Cooke
Children's Publisher: Anne O'Daly
Design Manager: Keith Davis
Designer: Melissa Roskell
Picture Manager: Sophie Mortimer

CONTENTS

Introduction

Mesopotamia—a region stretching from what is now Iraq to Syria and Turkey—was home to the world's first great civilizations.

Mesopotamia is the name given to the plain between the rivers Tigris and Euphrates. It was part of the so-called **Fertile** Crescent of the Middle East where the world's first cities emerged around seven thousand years ago. For over four thousand years, different peoples formed empires that covered various parts of the region. As each empire rose to power and then declined, the Sumerians, the Akkadians, the Assyrians, the Babylonians, and other peoples each dominated their neighbors.

Steps rise to the top of the Great Ziggurat of Ur. The ziggurats, or step-sided pyramids, towered over the cities of Mesopotamia.

This detail from a stone stela, or inscribed pillar, shows the Babylonian king Hammurabi (left) receiving the world's first set of laws from the god Shamash.

Meanwhile, the Mesopotamians made many technological advances. They used mud from the rivers to make bricks to build huge step-sided pyramids, called ziggurats, where they worshiped their gods. They invented the first form of writing, known as **cuneiform**, and used advanced math. The Mesopotamians were the first people to use the wheel for transportation, the first to people make glass, and the first civilization to have a formal code of laws.

This lion created from glazed tiles once adorned the walls surrounding the Ishtar Gate, a ceremonial entrance to the city of Babylon.

Strategic Position

One reason for Mesopotamia being the site of so many technological breakthroughs was its location. It lay where Africa and Asia met, with Turkish peoples to the north and the Egyptians to the west. New ideas were brought to the region from all sides of its borders.

Eventually, Mesopotamia's geographical position turned to its disadvantage. During a period of decline, it was invaded first by the mighty Persian Empire in the east and finally by the Macedonian Greek ruler Alexander the Great, who died in the city of Babylon in 323 BCE.

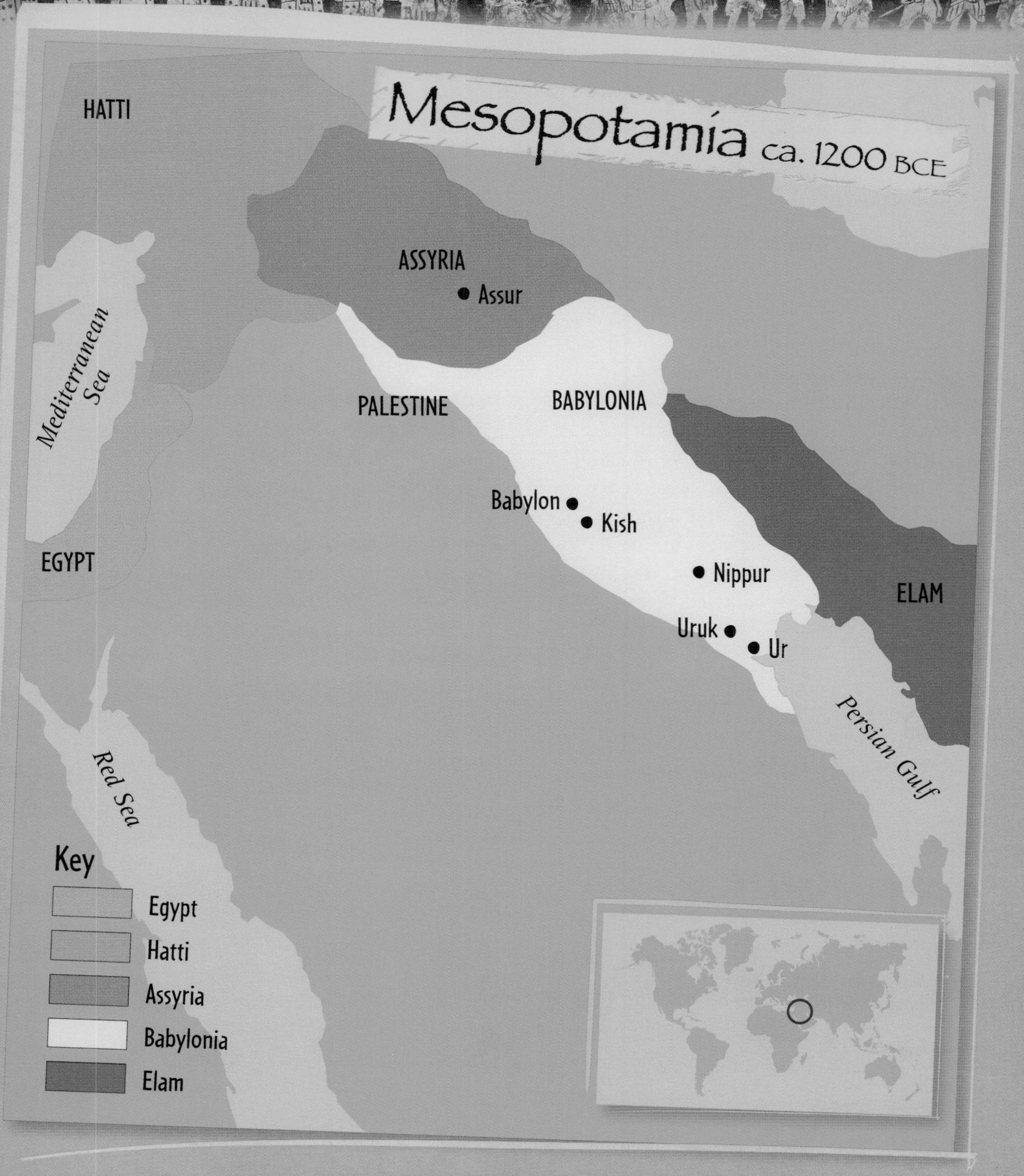

Mesopotamia ca. 1200 BCE

HATTI

ASSYRIA
● Assur

Mediterranean Sea

PALESTINE

BABYLONIA

EGYPT

Babylon ●
● Kish

● Nippur

ELAM

Uruk ●
● Ur

Persian Gulf

Red Sea

Key

Egypt

Hatti

Assyria

Babylonia

Elam

The Roots of the Empires

Around 12,000 BCE, early humans started to move into the plains between the Euphrates and Tigris Rivers in the so-called Fertile Crescent of West Asia.

At first these early humans lived as **nomads**, hunting game and gathering fruit for food. Then around 9000 BCE, for reasons that are not fully understood, they began to live in small settlements. They lived as **subsistence** farmers, growing crops and raising animals. These first farmers no longer had to hunt and gather their food. Having a regular food supply allowed them to plan their lives and developed communities.

The people used twigs and leaves to build small, round huts. They plowed the ground with sticks so they could plant wheat and barley. They later developed plows and harnessed their animals to pull them. They learned how to store grain in summer so they had food during the winter. They learned to grind grain into flour, which they baked with water to make bread. The people also **domesticated** animals to provide meat and milk.

The Euphrates was one of the two rivers that marked the borders of Mesopotamia, the "land between the rivers."

Men sharpen weapons while women clean animal skins in this artist's representation of an early Mesopotamian village.

These first farmers lived in what the ancient Greeks later named Mesopotamia, Greek for the "land between the rivers." There was very little rainfall in the region, so the early settlements depended on water from the Euphrates and the Tigris for their survival.

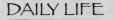

DAILY LIFE

The Plow

The development of the plow helped speed up the process by which Mesopotamians became farmers and settled in communities. Farmers originally used sticks as hoes to turn the earth for planting seeds, but around 6000 BCE they began to use a plow. At first they pulled the plow themselves, but later they used animals. That increased the area of land they could prepare for planting and so increased the amount of crops they could grow. That produced a surplus of food, which the farmers could then trade.

Modern workers make mud bricks in the desert using a method similar to that used by the ancient Mesopotamians.

DAILY LIFE

Eridu

At Eridu, on the Euphrates River in southern Mesopotamia, a village of mud bricks grew until by about 3000 BCE it had around four thousand inhabitants. Some historians claim that makes Eridu the oldest city in the world. The city expanded as a religious center dedicated to the worship of the god of water, Enki. A reliable water supply was vital to all the Mesopotamian empires.

Early Cultures

Around 7000 BCE, the Hassuna and Samarra cultures emerged. The people made pots from the clay that was found everywhere in the river plains. They used stone tools and they learned how to spin thread from the **flax** they grew and from the wool of the sheep and goats they kept. The people also made jewelry by carving small stones into beads.

After the Hassuna and Samarra, the Halaf dominated northern Mesopotamia for around six hundred years. The north was extremely fertile, with lots of rainfall. Farmers were able to grow a variety of food crops, including lentils and chickpeas.

Southern Mesopotamia

In the south, the Ubaid culture emerged around 5500 BCE and existed for about 1,500 years. The Ubaid people lived in settlements that gradually grew into small towns. Ubaid farmers produced more crops than they needed to feed their own population. They traded their surplus crops with their neighbors in return for natural resources they did not have, such as stone, wood, and metals.

The Ubaid were talented potters. They used clay from the Tigris and Euphrates to produce pots, which they decorated with distinctive **geometric** patterns in black and brown. As trading increased, the towns along the Euphrates and Tigris Rivers expanded. Eventually they became the world's first cities. These cities would bring great advances in the development of the region's civilizations.

This engraved stone tablet shows a cow (top right) and a plow below it. In the top left, a king stands before a temple.

DAILY LIFE

The Rise of Cities

The emergence of cities changed the way the Mesopotamians lived. In a city, they lived as a community. They spoke the same language, worshiped the same gods, and worked together to solve problems or defeat enemies. Leaders emerged among the urban communities, and society divided itself into groups. Each social group had a special role to perform. The wealthy acted as priests, the middle classes worked as merchants, and peasants worked as farmers.

The First Empires

The Sumerians were the first people to establish a successful empire in southern Mesopotamia. They made a huge advancement when they developed the world's first form of writing.

This carving of a man is covered in wedge-shaped writing known as cuneiform.

The Sumerians emerged around 3,500 BCE. They adapted their environment to the needs of the growing population. When they needed water to **irrigate** their crops, they built canals. They built barges to carry goods along the canals. When they needed to farm more land, they used oxen to pull their plows. They invented the wheel and made chariots—two-wheeled carts—pulled by donkeys. These allowed them to take goods to markets far away from home to trade. The Sumerians also developed a way to record details of their **transactions**. They invented a form of writing called cuneiform—"wedge-shaped." They used the potter's wheel to make pottery vessels, which they hardened by baking them in ovens called **kilns**.

City-States

The Sumerians lived in a series of separate **city-states** that included Uruk and Kish. Each city had its own ruler, the king. Rivalry

The remains of the Bit Resh temple have been excavated at the site of Uruk. The temple was built in the fourth millennium BCE.

between different kings caused frequent warfare, and cities rose and fell in power.

The first king to rule all Sumer was Etana of Kish, who ruled circa 2800 BCE. The city of Uruk took control when Meskiaggasher founded the First **Dynasty** of Uruk in around 2775 BCE. His son, Enmerkar (ruled ca. 2750 BCE), extended Uruk's power. It was during Emmerkar's reign that the Sumerians built the first ziggurats (step pyramids). Enmerkar was also the first king to write on clay tablets.

Legend or Reality?

Much of what we know about the Sumerian kings comes from stories written on clay tablets. Historians think these

DAILY LIFE

Uruk

The city of Uruk emerged around 4500 BCE. Its location between the Euphrates and Tigris rivers and close to a network of canals made it a major trade center. It expanded and became rich enough to support two temple complexes. One temple was dedicated to the sky god Anu and the other to the mother goddess Inanna. Uruk may also have been a political center for the emerging Sumerian Empire.

This stone carving from Assyria shows a hero—possibly a Mesopotamian ruler—overpowering a lion.

accounts are based on fact. The tablets record that the kings of Kish and the kings of Uruk alternately took control of the Sumerian Empire. One king we know about from a text found in the Akkadian city of Nineveh is Gilgamesh (see sidebar, opposite), the fifth king of Sumer. He ruled Uruk around 2700 BCE and built the city's walls. The story notes that many of Gilgamesh's actions angered the gods.

The First Dynasty of Ur

Around 2560 BCE Mesannepada, a prince of Kish, became the new ruler of Sumer and moved the empire's capital to Ur. He is said to have ruled for around

This board game was played in Ur around 2600–2400 BCE. Other similar games survive. This one was buried with a body in Ur's royal cemetery.

eighty years, but his long reign was followed by a series of weak rulers. The continual fighting between the city-states was weakening Sumer. The last ruler of Sumer was Lugalzagesi (ruled 2375–2350 BCE), king of Uruk, Kish, Umma, Ur, and Lagash. He hired soldiers from Akkad to fight in his army but they owed their loyalty to the Akkadian king, Sargon I. In 2334 BCE, the soldiers overthrew Lugalzagesi and replaced him with Sargon, ending the Sumerian Empire.

Sargon The Great

Sargon (ruled 2334–ca. 2271 BCE) ruled Akkad, to the northwest. Akkad, unlike Sumer, was a **centralized** state with its capital at Agade, on the Euphrates River. Sargon was an outstanding military **strategist** and commander. His armies fought and won thirty-four battles to

KEY PEOPLE

The Epic of Gilgamesh

The Epic of Gilgamesh was a poem about the popular Sumerian king Gilgamesh. It was told across Mesopotamia for centuries. Gilgamesh's adventures with his friend Enkidu, including their search for eternal life, were written down much later, in the seventh century CE. The story is recorded on a series of twelve clay tablets found in Nineveh. It tells of floods, demons, gods and goddesses, and the death of Enkidu.

Cuneiform

To record information to help run their empire, the Sumerians developed a system of writing on wet clay using reeds. The end of the reed pressed wedge shapes into the clay. This writing is known as cuneiform after the Latin word *cuneus* meaning "wedge." The first cuneiform tablets appeared around 3300 BCE and were used to record details about livestock and crops so farmers knew how much tax they owed.

increase his empire until the Akkadians controlled all of Mesopotamia and parts of what are now Syria, Turkey, and western Iran. Sargon also expanded the empire's trade beyond Mesopotamia. He imported lapis lazuli, a blue semiprecious stone, from Afghanistan and cedar wood from Lebanon, which was used for construction.

Akkadian Dynasty

The Akkadian Dynasty founded by Sargon ruled Mesopotamia for 141 years. At the peak of its power, Akkad controlled more than sixty-five cities. The Akkadians were constantly at war. They wanted to increase their empire, but as the empire grew its people became harder to control. People traveled around the empire by cart or

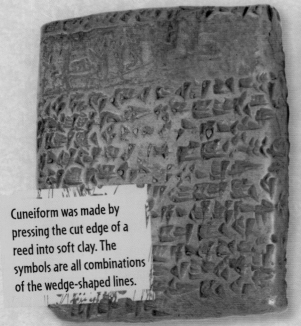

Cuneiform was made by pressing the cut edge of a reed into soft clay. The symbols are all combinations of the wedge-shaped lines.

The Akkadians carved cylinder seals (far left) to roll a pattern in soft clay (above). The clay hardened and formed a "signature" on documents.

riverboat, which made communications slow. In turn, that made it difficult to impose centralized order and gave Sargon's rivals a chance to rebel.

Akkadian Culture

Unlike the Sumerians, who spoke Sumerian, the Akkadians spoke Semitic, which was a language spoken by the Hebrews, Arabs, and Phoenicians. Sargon's rule in Sumer gave Mesopotamia two main cultures: Sumerian and Akkadian. The Sumerians learned to speak Semitic.

The Akkadians built palaces and temples. The most popular style of temple was the ziggurat, a stepped pyramid with a flat top (see sidebar, page 20).

DAILY LIFE

The Wheel

The Sumerians made a technological breakthrough around 3200 BCE when they invented the wheel. The first wheels were probably used horizontally to help potters throw pots. About three hundred years later, the wheel was turned sideways for use on vehicles. That step required advanced tools to create axles and holes to keep the wheels in place.

This bronze sculpture of the head of Sargon the Great was made around 2300–2215 BCE. It shows the elaborate beards worn by Akkadian men.

Sargon of Akkad

Sargon, the first king of the Akkad dynasty, ruled for fifty-six years. In Akkadian his name means "The True King," but his origins were humble. According to the Sumerian king list Sargon's father was a date-grower. Sargon built a new capital city at Akkad, which was probably close to the site of Babylon. He conquered Uruk, Ur, Umma, and Lagash in southern Mesopotamia. He was also known as the King of Kish.

The Akkadians were skilled sculptors. Their skills are most apparent in their cylinder seals. These were small rollers of limestone or ivory carved with a distinctive design, such as a picture. People rolled their personal cylinder across a soft clay seal to "sign" and authenticate documents.

End of the Akkadian Dynasty

Sargon's grandson, Naram-Sin (ruled 2254–2218 BCE), was an unpopular king who declared himself a god. Naram-Sin tore down the temple the goddess Inanna had built in Akkad when Sargon rose to power. According to legend, Enlil, the chief of the gods, sent the Gutians from the north to attack and conquer Akkad.

The ziggurat of Ur was restored as long ago as the sixth century BCE. It was restored again in the late twentieth century.

When Ur also revolted against Akkadian rule, the Akkadians lost control of Mesopotamia. Around 2004 BCE, however, a people named the Elamites from what is now western Iran **besieged** and defeated Ur, and massacred the population. The Elamite victory brought the Ur Dynasty to an end. For a century, the Mesopotamian city-states fought each other without any taking overall control.

Finally a new group—the Amorites, from present-day Syria—became dominant. They centralized their empire, taking

The Euphrates and Tigris Rivers

The two rivers of Mesopotamia made it possible for civilization to emerge. In spring, snowmelt filled the rivers, which overflowed and deposited fertile soil on their banks that made farming possible. The rivers also provided drinking water, fish, and a means of transportation. But unlike the Nile River in Egypt, neither the Euphrates nor the Tigris could be relied upon to flood regularly. The Mesopotamian peoples learned how to control the rivers' flow by building earth dikes to stop flooding and canals to irrigate fields.

Building the ziggurats required a huge amount of labor and materials, and the social organization to supply them.

Ziggurats

The most distinctive buildings of ancient Mesopotamia were ziggurats. These were flat-topped, stepped pyramids with a temple on the top. A ziggurat towered over each Mesopotamian city. The inner structure of the building was made from unbaked clay bricks while the outside was clad in bricks hardened in a kiln. Priests performed rituals in the temples, but ordinary people were not allowed to climb the buildings.

control of most of the territory that had been controlled by Sumer and Akkad. The Amorites chose Babylon as their capital, and became known as Babylonians.

The Babylonians believed their king was a god, and gave him total control over the empire. City-states in the empire no longer had any power. Everyone was **subject** to the supreme power of Babylon. The first Babylonian kings, who ruled from about 1900 to 1600 BCE, had little influence. That changed with the sixth king, Hammurabi (ruled 1792–1750 BCE).

Hammurabi

Hammurabi began his reign by going to war. He expanded his empire by defeating neighboring city-states and bringing them under his power. In 1787 BCE, he defeated Uruk. In 1763 BCE, he used a new tactic

Hammurabi's Code

Hammurabi is famous today for introducing the first known legal code to describe crimes and their punishments. The king claimed that the laws were given to him by the gods. Hammurabi engraved his laws on stone pillars throughout his empire. Breaking a law was considered a serious offense. Many of the crimes Hammurabi listed, such as stealing, were punishable by death. For other crimes, a criminal might be branded with hot metal or sent into exile.

when he dammed the Euphrates River to cut the water supply of Rim-Sin and force its surrender. As the Babylonian empire expanded, so did the tax revenues it received. As the empire became richer, Hammurabi constructed magnificent buildings and a network of canals. He ensured that his army was well fed and set up a system of stock keeping so that he knew how much grain and supplies were stored across the empire.

One of Hammurabi's most important contributions was to write a series of laws everyone had to follow. Hammurabi's Code listed what were considered crimes and what punishments they deserved. The laws were engraved on stone stele, or pillars, which were placed around the empire so that everyone could read them.

Hammurabi died in 1750 BCE. Only five more Babylonian kings ruled before the first Babylonian Empire came to an end.

This stone pillar from around 1790 BCE is inscribed with Hammurabi's legal code. At the top, the king receives the laws from the god Shamash.

New Empires

By 1600 BCE, the Babylonians had lost power in southern Mesopotamia. A new power arose in the north, the Hittites from what is now Turkey. New powers later emerged in the south.

This Hittite carving shows a mythical beast named a chimera, a winged lion with a human's head. The chimera seems to have been feared as an evil spirit.

Like earlier Mesopotamian peoples, the Hittites were farmers. They were skilled metal-workers whose superior-strength iron weapons helped them defeat their enemies and expand their empire. They also traded far beyond the Euphrates and Tigris Rivers to Iran in the east and the Arabian Peninsula in the south. At its peak, the Hittite Empire stretched from Turkey through parts of modern-day Syria and south along the coast of the Mediterranean Sea.

As they traded, the Hittites spread many aspects of Mesopotamian culture far beyond the region. They also adapted aspects of ancient Mesopotamian culture. They rewrote many of the laws in Hammurabi's Code, for example, to make them less severe.

The ruins of the former Hittite capital at Hattusa still stand on the plains of central Anatolia in Turkey.

The Kassites

While the Hittites controlled northern Mesopotamia, another foreign group gained control in the south. The origins of the Kassites are unclear, but they arrived in Mesopotamia as agricultural workers under the Babylonians. They rose up to rule Babylonia between around 1570 and 1170 BCE.

The Hittites had removed the statues of the god Marduk and his wife, Sarpanitum, from Babylon. The Kassite king Agum II (ruled ca.1595–1545 BCE) returned them, which made him popular with the Babylonians. The Kassites adopted the worship of Marduk and made Babylon their religious and ceremonial center. They also adopted many Babylonian customs and practices.

The Kassites preserved southern Mesopotamian culture through the second half of the second millennium BCE. They wrote down many ancient Mesopotamian myths and legends. After their empire collapsed, many Kassites stayed in Mesopotamia.

The Assyrians

The next people to build an empire in Mesopotamia were the Assyrians. Historians divide the Assyrian Empire into three periods: the Old Kingdom (1906–1392 BCE), the Middle Empire (1392–1014 BCE), and the Late Empire, or Neo-Assyrian Empire (911–609 BCE). Many Assyrian rulers were notable for the aggressive expansion of their empire through warfare.

This ancient carving shows Assyrian warriors with their horses. The coming of horses from Central Asia changed the nature of warfare.

Birth of Diplomacy

The Hittites introduced the Mesopotamians to a new way of settling disputes with enemies. In Mesopotamia, city-states usually solved disputes by going to war. After several inconclusive battles with Egypt, however, the Hittites signed a treaty with Egypt's King Rameses II. Both sides agreed to stop fighting and to respect each other's borders. They also agreed to work together if a third state invaded either of them. This idea of a defensive alliance is still used by nations today.

Military Expansion

The first Assyrian king, Ashur-Uballit I (ruled ca. 1365–1329 BCE), ruled an area between the Hittite and Kassite kingdoms. For over a hundred years the three cultures coexisted peacefully. But when Tukulti-Ninurta I (ruled ca. 1244–1207) became king, he had different ideas. He wanted to control all of Mesopotamia and attacked the Hittites, taking more than 28,000 prisoners of war.

Tiglath-Pileser I (ruled ca. 1115–1077 BCE), who was the greatest leader of the Middle Empire, extended Assyrian territory in Mesopotamia. He built a strong army and defeated tribes living in the

DAILY LIFE

Kassite Horses

The Kassites were the first Mesopotamians to breed horses successfully. The introduction of the horse from Central Asia coincided with the introduction of the chariot. Horses were mainly used to pull these two-wheeled carts in battle. Surviving Akkadian clay tablets contain extracts from a manual on training chariot horses. The text includes advice on diet and exercise.

Assyrian troops attack a city in Syria or Phoenicia in this detail from a **relief** carving from the first millennium BCE.

This nineteenthth-century drawing shows an ancient tablet that pictured archers from the army of Tiglath-Pileser II (ruled ca. 965–ca. 932 BCE).

Zagros Mountains to the east and the Aramaeans who lived in present-day Syria. He also rebuilt Assyria's farm-based economy to ensure that the empire stored spare grain in case of a future crop failure. He traded with the Phoenicians who lived along the Mediterranean coast in present-day Lebanon and Syria. The Phoenicians sent wood, glass, slaves, purple dye, and metals to Mesopotamia.

The Neo-Assyrian Empire

After a short period of reduced power, the kings of the Neo-Assyrian Empire continued to expand their territory while building new cities. Ashurnasirpal II (ruled 884–859 BCE) built a new capital at Nimrud on the Tigris River. He paid for the city with money collected from the people he conquered. Ashurnasirpal's cruelty and greed made him unpopular.

His son, Shalmaneser III (ruled 859–824 BCE), continued his father's aggressive expansion. He spent most of his reign at war. He fought tribespeople in the eastern mountains, the Babylonians, the Syrians, and the Egyptians. He also invaded Israel. Despite the **booty** he seized and his victories, he was also an unpopular ruler. The Assyrian people resented the high taxes they had to pay to fund his wars and frequently tried to overthrow him.

The Discovery of Nimrud

Under Ashurnasirpal II, the Assyrian capital Nimrud was noted for its temples and palaces, its gardens, and its zoo. In 706 BCE, however, the capital moved back to Ashur. Nimrud was abandoned and its location was lost. The British archeologist Max Mallowan found it by accident in 1957. Exploring in Iraq, he found a brick stamped with the name of Shalmaneser III. The brick led to the rediscovery of the whole city.

This carving from Nineveh is thought to show Ashur, who was the chief god of the Assyrians and who may have represented the sun.

The Nergal Gate, once the main entrance into Nineveh, was excavated in the nineteenth century and rebuilt in the twentieth century.

Sargon II

A new dynasty began when Sargon II seized power from King Shalmaneser V around 722 BCE. Sargon (ruled ca. 722–705 BCE) modeled his name and style of rule on Sargon I, the former king of Akkad. Sargon II divided the vast Assyrian empire into seventy provinces. Governors controlled each province and reported back to Sargon.

In 720 BCE the Chaldeans from the west formed an alliance with the Elamites and conquered Babylonia. Sargon II continued to invade his other neighbors, however. Eventually, he controlled an area that stretched from Egypt in the south, west to the Mediterranean, and into the Zagros Mountains to the east.

DAILY LIFE

Nineveh

Nineveh was one of the oldest and most spectacular of Mesopotamian cities. It grew wealthy from its position on a major trade route on the Tigris River. At its height under Sennacherib (ruled 705–681 BCE), Nineveh had a population of around 150,000 and covered 2.9 square miles (750 hectares). The city had wide streets, public squares, and a brick-built aqueduct that provided fresh water. Around the palace were gardens with rare plants from across the empire.

Sargon II's huge army was extremely expensive to maintain. He constantly needed extra money and relied on captured gold and silver. Although he built himself a new palace and city—the Fortress of Sargon—he died in battle before the building was completed.

More Palaces and Wars

Sargon II's son, Sennacherib (ruled 705–681 BCE) moved the capital back to Ashur, the traditional capital of Assyria, before moving it again to Nineveh in 701 BCE. He continued to use warfare to increase Assyrian territory. By the time his son, Esarhaddon, became king in 681 BCE,

Assyrian Warfare

The Assyrians based their economy on seizing goods and slaves in warfare. They kept detailed records of their campaigns. The Assyrians fought every spring and summer, after the harvest was stored. The 100,000-strong army was largely made up of farmers who carried weapons such as spears, bows and arrows, slings, swords, and axes. Horse-drawn chariots carried archers close to the enemy soldiers.

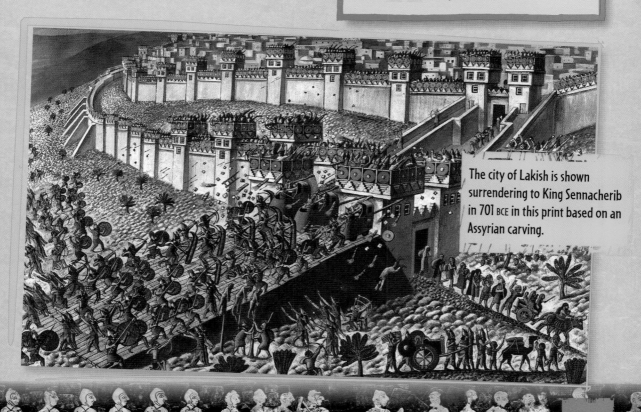

The city of Lakish is shown surrendering to King Sennacherib in 701 BCE in this print based on an Assyrian carving.

King Ashurbanipal (with dish) makes offerings to the Assyrian gods. Keeping the gods happy was one of the king's most important duties.

Conquest of Egypt

In 671 BCE, Esarhaddon led his army across the Sinai Desert to the Nile Delta in Egypt. According to his account, it took the Assyrians just two weeks to defeat the Egyptian army and conquer the capital at Memphis. The size of Egypt and its distance from Mesopotamia, however, made it difficult to integrate Egypt fully into the Assyrian Empire. It was not long before the Egyptians had retaken Memphis.

the Assyrian Empire covered most of what is now the Middle East. Esarhaddon added Egypt, Sidon (a city in Lebanon), and parts of Palestine. By 670 BCE, the empire was so large it was almost ungovernable. Sennacherib's sons divided it. While Shamash-shumi-ukin became king of Babylonia, another son, Ashurbanipal, became king of Assyria in 669 BCE.

Ashurbanipal

Although the Assyrian nobles despised Ashurbanipal (ruled ca. 669–627 BCE), he was the last great ruler of Assyria. By then, the Assyrian Empire stretched from modern-day Turkey east to Iran and west into Egypt. Ashurbanipal decided to let local leaders rule rather than imposing

Assyrian leaders on them. But this did not stop his subjects rebelling. The Egyptians drove the Assyrians out, after which the two empires became trading partners. This benefited Assyria, because Egypt was too far away to control effectively. When his brother Shamash-shumi-ukin tried to overthrow him, Ashurbanipal attacked Babylon and defeated him.

As well as being a military leader, Ashurbanipal was well educated. He founded the first library in Mesopotamia. After Ashurbanipal's death, Assyria's power declined. It was soon taken over by a new power, the New Babylonian Empire.

The Flood Tablet from the Library of Ashurbanipal tells the story of how Gilgamesh survives a great flood.

KEY PEOPLE

Ashurbanipal's Library

Ashurbanipal collected between twenty thousand and thirty thousand cuneiform tablets in one of the first known libraries. The tablets were Sumerian, Akkadian, Babylonian, and Assyrian texts, including the epic poem Gilgamesh. The library was stored in Nineveh, organized by subject. The subjects included science and poetry, as well as government papers that gave details of military campaigns. Archeologists rediscovered the library in 1852 and much of what is known about ancient Mesopotamia is based on its contents.

The New Babylonians

Nearly a thousand years after the death of Hammurabi, Babylon took control of Mesopotamia once again. Historians describe this recovery as the Neo-Babylonian, or "new" Babylonian, period.

During the Neo-Babylonian Empire (626–539 BCE) King Nabopolassar (ruled 626–605 BCE) and his son Nebuchadnezzar (ruled 605–562 BCE) made Babylon the richest and largest city in the world. Although the Neo-Babylonian Empire lasted less than a century, its cultural achievements outshone those of earlier and later Mesopotamian cultures.

Nabopolassar

In 626 BCE the Chaldean prince Nabopolassar defeated the Assyrian army at Uruk and captured the throne of Babylon. Nabopolassar now led a ten-year struggle to rid the rest of the region of the hated Assyrians. Nabopolassar later formed an alliance with Cyaxeres, king of the Medes of what is now Iran, to get rid of the Assyrian dynasty. Together, they besieged the Assyrian capital at Nineveh in 612 BCE. After a three-month siege, Nineveh fell and Nabopolassar destroyed the city. The Medes returned to their home on the Iranian plateau, leaving Nabopolassar to reign as king of Mesopotamia.

The Egyptian Threat

With the Assyrians defeated, the Egyptians saw a chance to recapturee the Mediterranean coast of Syria–Palestine, the region that stretched from the Nile Delta north toward present-day Turkey.

The ruins of Babylon were restored in the late twentieth century but were later abandoned during the wars in Iraq.

The Babylonian sun god chases away a monster named Chaos in this drawing of an ancient carving.

The Babylonians, however, relied on the regions for natural resources such as metals and for access to the Mediterranean coast. Nabopolassar sent his son, Nebuchadnezzar, to stop the Egyptians. In 605 BCE Nebuchadnezzar, who was a skilled soldier, surprised the Egyptian army at Karkamish and defeated them, winning control of Syria-Palestine. He planned to march on Egypt itself, but news reached him of his father's death.

Battle of Karkamish

The 605 BCE Battle of Karkamish changed the ancient world. Nebuchadnezzar destroyed the Egyptian and Assyrian armies. Many of the Egyptians fled, but the Babylonians pursued them. Babylonian records claim that no Egyptians survived.

In this Roman carving, Babylonians are shown carrying off treasures after the fall of the Jewish capital at Jerusalem.

DAILY LIFE

Trade

Early trade was carried out by barter, or swapping goods for other goods, but by the Babylonian period people had started to use metal as a form of money. It was easier to use a silver bar for payment than, say, a cow. Soon after money appeared, moneylenders also appeared. Workers could borrow against their labor and farmers could borrow against their grain. A debt had to be repaid with interest within an agreed period.

He raced back to Babylon to prevent anyone else seizing his throne. He became Nebuchadnezzer II.

Nebuchadnezzar II

Nebuchadnezzar's reign was the high point of Mesopotamian culture, surpassing even the reign of Hammurabi. Nebuchadnezzar was a supreme military leader who led his army into many battles to increase territory and to raise money for the empire. But he was also a builder who made Babylon the most magnificent city of the ancient world. He constructued one of the Seven Wonders of the ancient world: the Hanging Gardens.

In 601 BCE Nebuchadnezzar marched against Egypt once again. He hoped to conquer the Nile Valley as the Assyrians had done a century earlier, but he failed and was forced to return to Babylon. Nebuchadnezzar never succeeded in conquering Egypt, but when the small kingdom of Judah refused to pay tax to Babylonia, hoping Egypt would support it, Nebuchadnezzar's troops surrounded Jerusalem, its capital. In 597 BCE the city fell to the Babylonians, who emptied it of much of its wealth. When Judah rebelled again a few years later, the Babylonians besieged Jerusalem for eighteen months. In 587 BCE, the city fell. The Babylonians destroyed much of the city, including the Temple of Solomon, which had been the most important building in Judah. Nebuchadnezzar took many of Judah's Jewish population into exile in Bablyon. The exile lasted over sixty years and remains an infamous period of suffering in the history of the Jewish people.

Babylon's Height

Nebuchadnezzar used the treasure he seized in his military campaigns to rebuild and expand Babylon. He enlarged Esagila, the temple of Marduk. He also enlarged Etemenanli, the tallest mud-brick ziggurat

Babylonian Math

The Babylonians used a counting system based on the number sixty. This is why there are sixty seconds in a minute and sixty minutes in an hour. Babylonian mathematicians were also advanced in algebra and had worked out advanced mathematical theorems, or rules. They used a set of tables for complex calculations but they did not understand geometry.

Babylonian cities were propserous places with an economy based on using a form of money.

The Hanging Gardens

The Hanging Gardens of Babylon were a series of terraces that rose up like a green mountain. They were said to be about 400 feet (122 meters) square and 80 feet (24 m) high. To water the trees, plants, and vines, engineers built a complex system of buckets, pulleys, and cords to carry water from the Euphrates. Nothing remains of the gardens, but ancient tablets describe them in detail.

in Mesopotamia. Etemenanli may have inspired the famous Bible story of the Tower of Babel. Nebuchadnezzar extended the city walls and covered them with **glazed** bricks that shone in the sunlight. He built a new main entrance to the city, the magnificent Ishtar Gate. He built the spectacular Hanging Gardens for his wife, Amytis. It was said that he wanted to prevent her feeling homesick for her mountainous native land to the north.

Under Nebuchadnezzar, Babylon became a center of learning and culture. Educated men discussed **astronomy**, religion, math, and literature. They recorded their

This reconstruction of the Hanging Gardens suggests one possible way in which a system of pulleys raised water up a central shaft.

This tiled image of an auroch—an ancient form of cow—decorated the walls of Babylon's Ishtar Gate.

debates in cuneiform on clay tablets. Religion was an essential part of daily life. There were thousands of gods, although the Babylonians only worshiped the few they hoped would help them in their daily lives. The most important of these gods was Marduk, who had originally been the city's chief god. The highlight of the religious year was the annual spring festival (Akitu), which lasted for eleven days and celebrated the rebirth of nature.

The Babylonian economy continued to rely on agriculture, and most Babylonians worked on the land. The most important crops were barley and wheat, and grain was the staple food of everyone except

The Ishtar Gate

Nebuchadnezzar wanted any visitor to Babylon to be impressed by the wealth of the city. Around 575 BCE he built the Ishtar Gate as the main entrance through the city's inner walls. It was highly decorated. The gate's walls were covered with blue glazed bricks decorated with alternate rows of bulls, lions, and dragons made from yellow and brown tiles. The name Ishtar came from a Babylonian goddess.

Tower of Babel

The Bible tells how ancient people who all spoke the same language wanted to build a tower to reach up to God in the sky. To punish them, God was said to have made the builders all speak in different languages. The people then spread the languages to different parts of the world. In the Bible, the tower is called Babel. Historians believe that the original version of the tower in the story might have been the ziggurat dedicated to Marduk in Babylon.

the very richest Babylonians, who could afford meat. Skilled craftsmen were highly valued in Babylon, such as brickmakers, potters, and metalworkers.

With its wide streets, its canals, and its ordered society, Babylon was the most magnificent city the world had ever seen. After Nebuchadnezzar died, however, the city was ruled by a series of short-lived kings who achieved little of note.

Nabonidus

The last of the Babylonian kings was Nabonidus (ruled ca. 556–539 BCE). He was a former official of Nebuchadnezzar who came to power after a **palace coup** that overthrew King Labashi-Marduk.

The Ishtar Gate was a ceremonial entrance through the inner walls that protected Babylon from attack.

In 1563 the artist Pieter Brueghel painted this version of the Tower of Babel. The real building was probably a stepped ziggurat.

Nabonidus claimed that he did not want power himself, but he was encouraged to seize the throne by his scheming mother and his ambitious son, Belshazzar, who wanted the throne for himself.

Nabonidus was an unpopular ruler. He lived in Tayma, an **oasis** in northwestern Arabia, leaving Belshazzar to rule Babylon. Nabonidus also changed the empire's official religion from the worship of Marduk to the worship of the moon

god, Sin. He removed statues of Marduk from Babylon, which made him even more unpopular with the Babylonians.

Nabonidus stayed in Tayma for around ten years. He was trying to expand Babylonian power in Arabia because it was no longer possible to expand into the areas Babylon had formely exploited in northern Mesopotamia, Turkey, and Iran. A powerful new enemy now controlled those regions: the Persians.

The End of the Empires

The end of the Mesopotamian empires came with the rise of a new power in the region. The Persians were a people from beyond the Zagros Mountains to the east, in present-day Iran.

The Persian king Cyrus returns sacred treasures to the Jews after releasing them from their long exile in Babylon.

The Persians had been growing in strength in their homeland and expanding their territory. Eventually their spread westward threatened the valley of the Tigris and Euphrates Rivers. In 550 BCE, not long after the death of King Nebuchadnezzar in Babylon, Cyrus II (ruled ca. 559–530 BCE) became king in Ashan in western Persia. In just ten years of military campaigns Cyrus would created a Persian Empire that stretched from the Aegean Sea of Greece as far east as India.

Cyrus Expands the Empire

Cyrus was one of the ancient world's most outstanding military leaders whose campaigns conquered many lands. Unlike many earlier Mesopotamian rulers, Cyrus treated the peoples he conquered with great respect and allowed them to keep their traditions and religion. Cyrus put military governors (known as satraps) in charge of each

Cyrus ruled his empire from his capital at Pasargadae, which stood in what is now Iran, near the modern city of Shiraz.

province. The satraps were allowed to rule independently. In return, Cyrus's only requirement was that they should collect and send taxes to his treasury and they also had to provide men to serve in the Persian army.

Invasion of Babylon

As he expanded west, Cyrus wanted to conquer the Neo-Babylonian Empire. By around 540 BCE, Babylonia and its kingdoms—Syria, Judea, Phoenicia, and parts of Arabia—were the only part of the Middle East Cyrus had not defeated. Babylonia was surrounded by Persian territory on three sides. The Babylonian king Nabonidus had tried to make alliance with the kingdom of Lydia, in what is

KEY PEOPLE

Cyrus the Great

The Persian emperor Cyrus was an outstanding leader of the ancient world. He ruthlessly conquered vast territories and kingdoms, but won the goodwill of those he conquered by leaving their political and religious institutions intact. This behavior often led to his being seen as a liberator rather than a conqueror. His success came to an end when he was killed in battle against the Massagetai of Central Asia in 530 BCE.

The Cyrus Cylinder tells how the king captured Babylon with the help of Marduk, whom Cyrus restored to his place as the city's chief god.

The Cyrus Cylinder

The Cyrus Cylinder is made from clay and covered with cuneiform. It gives Cyrus's account of his conquest of Babylon in 539 BCE. Cyrus describes how he defeated Babylon with the help of the god Marduk and how he set free the Jews. The cylinder grants rights to the Babylonians, and has been called the first declaration of human rights. In fact, Cyrus was behaving like many new rulers who introduced reforms.

now Turkey, to fight together against Persia. The alliance failed, however, and Babylonia faced the Persians alone.

Defeat at Opis

Cyrus began his invasion of Babylonia by making an alliance with Gobryas, who was a Babylonian governor who controlled a region named Gutium. In around September 539 BCE, the Persian army met the Babylonian army at Opis, a crossing place on the Tigris River about 50 miles (80 kilometers) north of modern-day Baghdad in Iraq. Details of the fighting have been lost, but the Babylonians suffered a complete defeat and Belshazzar was killed. The Babylonian army is never mentioned again in any accounts: it simply ceased to exist.

End of the Empires

In October 539 BCE Gobryas marched into Babylon unopposed. A few days later, Cyrus arrived. He freed the Jews who had been living in **exile** in Babylon since Nebuchadnezzar had destroyed Jerusalem sixty years earlier. He restored the cult of Marduk and arranged for the return of the statues of gods that had been removed by Nabonidus. Cyrus's actions made him popular with many of his Mesopotamian subjects, but the Persian conquest marked the end of the great empires of Sumer, Assyria, and Babylon.

Alexander the Great

After Cyrus, Babylon started to decline. An influx of Persian immigrants saw the rise of the Aramaic language instead of Babylonian Semitic, although temple scribes kept the cuneiform script alive. The Macedonian leader Alexander overthrew the Persians in 331 BCE. He loved Babylon and planned to restore it to its former glory. He died there in 323 BCE before his plans came to anything.

This wall frieze shows the elite warriors of the Persian army. Cyrus depended on their fighting skills for his success.

Timeline

ca. **5000** BCE   The first towns and cities emerge in Sumer. Sumerian farmers dig canals to irrigate their fields.

ca. **4000** BCE   Powerful Sumerian city-states build ziggurats (stepped pyramids) as temples to their gods.

ca. **3500** BCE   Southern Mesopotamian is dominated by Sumerian city-states, including Ur, Uruk, Eridu, Kish, Lagash, and Nippur.

ca. **3300** BCE.   The Sumerians develop the world's first writing system, named cuneiform.

ca. **3200** BCE   The Sumerians adapt the potter's wheel and use it on vehicles.

ca. **2700** BCE   Gilgamesh becomes king of the city-state of Ur.

ca. **2400** BCE   The rising influence of the Akkadians is reflected in the replacement of Sumerian by Akkadian as the main language of Mesopotamia.

ca. **2330** BCE   The Akkadian King Sargon the Great conquers many Sumerian city-states to create the Akkadian Empire.

ca. **2254** BCE   Under King Naram-Sin, the Akkadian Empire reaches its greatest extent.

ca. **2100** BCE   The Akkadian Empire declines and the Sumerians reemerge, rebuilding the city of Ur, which is later conquered by the Elamites.

ca. 1900 BCE	The Assyrians of central Turkey rise to power in northern Mesopotamia.
1792 BCE	Hammurabi becomes king of Babylon. He will conquer the Assyrian Empire and write the world's first law code.
1750 BCE	After the death of Hammurabi, Babylon begins a long period of decline; in 1595 it is conquered by the Kassites.
1250 BCE	The reemergence of the Assyrians is quickened when they begin to make iron tools and weapons.
1225 BCE	The Assyrians overthrow Babylon.
1115 BCE	The Second Assyrian Empire reaches its peak under King Tiglath-Pileser I, but goes into decline after his death.
722 BCE	The Akkadian King Sargon II takes the throne of Assyria.
709 BCE	Sargon II captures Babylon.
701 BCE	After Sargon II dies, Sennacherib moves the capital from Babylon to Nineveh.
669 BCE	Ashurbanipal becomes king of Assyria. He will be the last great ruler; after his death in 627 BCE the empire will crumble.
612 BCE	Nabopolassar takes control of Babylon from the Assyrians and begins the Neo-Babylonian (New Babylonian) Empire.
605 BCE	Nebuchadnezzar begins his fifty-year rule of Babylon, during which the city will reach its peak.
539 BCE	Cyrus the Great conquers Babylon, and Mesopotamia becomes part of the Persian Empire.

Glossary

astronomy The study of the movement of bodies in the heavens, such as stars and planets.

besieged Surrounded and cut off a place in order to force it to surrender.

booty Valuable goods that are stolen by an army during wartime.

centralized A system in which power is concentrated in a central authority.

city-state A state formed by a city and its surrounding territory.

cuneiform A kind of writing made by pressing a wedge-shaped needle into soft clay.

domesticated Describes plants or animals that are grown as crops or raised for food.

dynasty A series of rulers who are members of the same family.

exile The state of being barred from one's home country, usually as a form of punishment.

fertile Capable of producing many crops.

flax A blue-flowered plant whose fibers make a textile called linen.

geometric Having regular lines and shapes.

glazed Describes pottery, bricks, or tiles that have a thin, shiny coating.

irrigate To supply water to an area in order to grow crops.

kiln An oven for baking pottery to harden it.

nomads People who travel from place to place and have no permanent home.

oasis An isolated area of vegetation around a water source in a desert.

palace coup An illegal attempt to seize the throne made by people who are closely linked to the current ruler.

relief A carving in which a design stands out from a flat surface.

strategist A person who is skilled in making long-term plans.

subject Describes a country that is under the authority of another.

subsistence Describes a lifestyle in which people have just enough food to survive.

transactions Exchanges that involve buying and selling things.

Further Reading

Books

Dalal, Anita. *Ancient Mesopotamia.*
Facts at Your Fingertips. Redding, CT:
Brown Bear Books, 2009.

Kuiper, Kathleen. *Mesopotamia: The
World's Earliest Civilization.* The
Britannica Guide to Ancient
Civilizations. New York: Rosen
Education Service, 2010.

Nardo, Don. *Life and Worship in
Ancient Mesopotamia.* Lucent Library
of Historical Eras. Detroit, MI: Lucent
Books, 2009.

Oakes, Lorna. *Mesopotamia.* Passport to
the Past. New York: Rosen Publishing
Group, 2009.

Somervill, Barbara A. *Empires of
Ancient Mesopotamia.* Great Empires
of the Past. New York: Chelsea House
Publishers, 2010.

Websites

British Museum
www.mesopotamia.co.uk
The British Museum's interactive
website about ancient Mesopotamia,
with many artifacts.

Encyclopedia of Ancient History
www.ancient.eu/Mesopotamia
Articles about the civilizations of
Mesopotamia from the *Encyclopedia of
Ancient History.*

Time Maps
www.timemaps.com/civilization
Ancient-Mesopotamia
A timemap of ancient Mesopotamia
with links to various articles.

University of Chicago
mesopotamia.lib.uchicago.edu
A Mesopotamia website from the
Oriental Institute at the University of
Chicago, with links to many artifacts.

Publisher's note to educators and parents: Our editors have carefully reviewed these websites to ensure
that they are suitable for students. Many websites change frequently, however, and we cannot guarantee
that a site's future contents will continue to meet our high standards of quality and educational value.
Be advised that students should be closely supervised whenever they access the Internet.

Index